DOMINIC HODGSON

WALK
YOURSELF
WEALTHY

The quick, easy and no-BS guide to transform your passion
for pooches into an insanely profitable and fun dog
walking empire

Published by

Elite Publishing Academy

Tel: 0800 6890548

www.ElitePublishingAcademy.com

First Edition published 2018
© Dominic Hodgson 2018

Printed and bound in Great Britain by

Elite Publishing Academy

www.ElitePublishingAcademy.com

A catalogue record for this book
is available from The British Library

ISBN **978-1-910090-71-8**

WHAT DOG WALKERS ARE SAYING ABOUT
WALK YOURSELF WEALTHY

"This book will give you everything you need to overtake the competition and start making more money with your business. Dom has done a great job of fitting a lot of great information into a small book and, of course, in his signature, humorous writing style. Now all that is left for you to do is take in that knowledge and implement it."
Nick Benger – Bark, Play, Teach
www.barkplayteach.com

"As a pet business owner who was doing OK and with ambitions way beyond earning a few quid an hour, I spent a long time researching successful pet business owners to see what they were doing. I became aware of Dom initially through social media and was attracted to how he marketed his business. After signing up for Dom's 33 ideas, I was hooked and was even more keen to learn how he became the UK's number-one dog adventure company.

When I read *Walk Yourself Wealthy* my first thoughts were I can't believe he's sharing all this valuable information so others can improve their businesses. Being selfish, I want to be the number-one dog service provider in my town and didn't want anyone else learning Dom's secrets to his success. Then I realised I'm in a great position to be the first to implement all of this and nab all the best clients first where others would be too scared. It really is a case of having the balls, or ladyballs as Dom would say, to make difficult decisions which will benefit your business massively not only in the long term but as soon as you get started.

I'm only at the beginning of working through Dom's tips and have attracted two new premium clients. Other walkers are already asking me questions, but I know they won't be prepared to put in the hard work like I have, and I'm not sharing information with people who don't want to buy this book.

Thanks to Dom, I have big plans for the future, and by following the advice and tips in *Walk Yourself Wealthy* from someone who has actually been there and done that, I'm confident I'll soon be the go-to person in my area overtaking those who have been in business for many years.

If you're happy plodding along charging the same as everyone else in your town and happy doing four plus walks a day to scrape by, this is probably not the book for you. *Walk Yourself Wealthy* is a five-star read for those ambitious pet business owners who are not scared of hard work and ruffling a few feathers along the way!"
Karen Rhodes – Suffolk Dog Services
www.suffolkdogservices.co.uk

"I found Dom's *Walk Yourself Wealthy* book easy to read (no jargon to translate), very informative and packed full of ideas that are relatively easy to implement into my own business. I am looking forward to reading it again and am sure I will refer back to it many times in the future."
Debbie Potter – Potter Paws Dog Walking
www.potterpaws.co.uk

"Fantastic read, I've been working hard since reading this bible, and I've still got a huge 'to do' list. I blame Dominic Hodgson for motivating my work ethic!

Thank you Dom for giving me a head full of ideas and a kick up the arse!"
Sandy Sharma – The K9 Carers
www.thek9carers.com

"Dominic Hodgson's new book *Walk Yourself Wealthy* is a must for anyone wishing to start up or develop their existing dog walking business but find themselves stuck in a rut or unsure how to go about making changes.

I came across Dom a few months ago when my pet care business was at a make-or-break point. I wasn't earning enough to make it a full-time business, and I desperately needed to attract more customers – but not just any customers; to increase my prices; and to fine tune my business. I had no idea where to even start with any of it, so I signed up for Dom's 'Grow Your Pet Business FAST Profit Kickstarter' webinars, which set me off on the right track. *Walk Yourself Wealthy* not only reinforces what I learnt on the webinars, but also offers much more in the way of practical, easy-to-follow, no-nonsense advice with the emphasis on effective marketing strategies.

Walk Yourself Wealthy has armed me with the tools, knowledge and insight to improve and grow my business with unlimited potential. How far I take it is now up to me, and having already implemented some of what I have learnt so far, I am beginning to reap the benefits. Certainly to be the best is to learn from the best!"
Sheena Dunlop – Paws First Pet Care
www.pawsfirstpetcare.co.uk

"I had already signed up for Dom's 33 tips emails, and found them interesting, but knew there was a lot more involved than what had been said in the emails, so signed up for the Profit Kickstarter webinars – I was interested in what he had to say, but was also not convinced that it could work for my business, as a small fish in a very large pond of dog walkers in my area. When I had set up a year ago, I had in my mind a business that was different from other walkers in the area, but a year in had found myself being just like the others, with no idea how to be different enough to bring the clients in. The Profit Kickstarter does exactly what it says – it gave me a kick to get on and do something about it! So I've implemented some of Dom's advice, immediately putting my prices up, and rewording my website to (hopefully!) stand out from the crowd, and have some other ideas I want to implement over the coming weeks to make my business into the vision I had in the beginning. Well worth the money if you need advice (and a kick!) to get things moving!"

Maxine Simmonds – A Walk In The Park
www.awalkintheparkstockport.co.uk

"I was the sceptical woman, reading what Dom was saying but not quite believing it would work for me. Surely I couldn't charge more than my competitors? I'd only been trading less than a year! But reading what Dom wrote made a lot of sense to me – I knew I was good at what I do and I knew I was worth it! So I put my prices up, tried some lead generating marketing and hey presto – two new clients within a week! I've been trusting Dom's advice for a couple of months now and business is going great (to the extent I'm currently employing someone to help me with the increased work load!!).

My advice would be: trust in Dom and trust in yourself! If you know you're great at what you do, market it! Thank you

Dom for all your advice – I will be signing up for more..."
Tammie Kirk – Clan Canines, Edinburgh
www.clancanines.co.uk

"I have been in business for seven years and I thought old dogs can't learn new tricks. But despite having many years' experience, I have found I can still learn more about marketing my pet business, which is needed, especially in today's competitive dog walking market.

What attracted me first to this book was that Dom talks about premium pricing; so many new businesses undercut then fail, and I liked that this book was focusing on premium pricing in one of the chapters. In this book, it states, business is business the world over and people always buy the things they want; you just need to make sure your business is the one they want to buy from. This book can help you be the one the clients choose.

Dom explains why pricing matters and how higher prices mean less work, as fewer clients to deal with. I trust him as from my experience he is so right; so many dog walkers are making the mistake of going way too cheap and discounting so was encouraging to see him talk about premium pricing for a profitable business.

If you are wondering how to get new clients to pick you, this book can give you ideas to make them pick your company. Dom talks about going niche and this helped me decide on something I have been thinking about, how to make my business different; I am going to specialise in small dogs. Size now matters in my new business marketing. He gives other ideas such as specialising in one type of dog, and this would work well if you loved Labs or, say, cocker spaniels. A great idea to attract a breed of dog client to your dog walking business, so many great ideas for niching in your business.

Week in, week out, more and more dog walking companies are opening up everywhere, so you really need to make your business more unique to stand out from the crowd, and this book is great for giving you different ideas.

Dom also gives great ideas on using lead generation marketing. This is something I have not used before in my business and I plan to try it out.

This book has lots of personality in it, and it had me hooked and wanting to learn more from the start. I started reading it at bedtime and before I knew it was 1 am as I wanted to finish the book. It's a long time since I read a whole book in one sitting. I didn't want to go to sleep, feeling I would miss something. This is a great book for giving you the key marketing foundations you need. I will be purchasing more products from Dom and will be joining his inner circle to learn more.

I hope you enjoy the book as much as I did."
Fiona Wheater – Edinburgh Pet Services
www.edinburghpetservices.co.uk

"*Walk Yourself Wealthy* is a fantastic 'grow your business fast' type guide for any aspiring dog walker, written by someone who's 'been there' and 'done it'.

The thing is with Dom, he's not your average dog walker.

Not because he's been born with special skills or just been abnormally lucky – he's not your average dog walker because he's relentlessly trying different marketing strategies and techniques, to see what works and what doesn't. This book, while short, contains that knowledge and everything you need to know to become the 'top dog' in your industry. Follow everything in this book to the letter, and you'll have people queuing up at your doorstep.

Every chapter is gold, from being premium to being inaccessible – the way Dom talks you through these subjects means anyone can start to grow their dog walking business fast.

If you're a dog walker, I couldn't recommend this book highly enough. This is a must-read."
Ben Waters
www.woofwebsites.co.uk

"Am I qualified to write a review? I don't have a dog walking business; I don't even have a dog. Yet. But actually, if you read Dom's book you will find neither matters.

I do actually have a business; much like Dom teaches pet business owners how to grow their businesses, I teach salon owners how to grow their salons.

We teach the same thing. How can that be? Surely, the two businesses are different? They're not. Business and marketing principles are the same, whether you are selling adventures to cocker spaniel owners, or highlights to yummy mummies. Because you are selling to people. And selling to people is what Dom is an expert in. If you heed his advice and take action with the information he shares in this easy-to-read, entertaining book, you can become the expert too.

This shit works. I know because I've done it myself (yes, even written two books), and the salon owners I work with have done it, and I've seen what Dom does and how it works for him and his clients. Let it work for you too, and be the go-to dog walker in your patch."

Kat Smith
www.growyoursalonfast.com

"Listen to Dom – he knows his stuff! If you're serious about making more money from your dog walking business, I can say, hand on heart as a marketing consultant, the principles and strategies *Walk Yourself Wealthy* steps you through are bang on the money. But can you trust Dom's advice? Yes! Because it's no fluke he's the most sought-after pet business coach in the UK. Which means you'd be barking mad not to listen."

Kathryn Reid – Marketing Expert
www.websitewords.co.nz

"You may be thinking to yourself: 'My dog walking business is doing OK; why do I need this guy's book?'

And your business may well be doing okay… for now.

But businesses, all businesses, need constant care and attention, just like puppies. Give a puppy care, feed them well and train them properly and you will have something in your life that brings you joy every day. Don't care for a puppy properly, and you will have a miserable, joyless life together.

Businesses are exactly the same.

Now is a great time to have a dog walking business. Business is booming, isn't it? But that won't last forever.

Why? Because very soon, every man and his dog (sorry) will be in the dog walking business. And your local town will have dozens of doggy walkers all cutting each other's throats to get a slice of YOUR business.

Which is why you need Dom's book. When the time comes that Tom, Dick and Harry are desperately dogfighting for scraps of business, YOU will have a business you love being in, that brings you joy and freedom and that feeds and looks after itself.

Better than that, YOU will have a business that doesn't just do 'OK'. YOUR doggy business will ROCK! You will have dog owners queuing at YOUR door, desperate to pay you more money than Tom, Dick and Harry combined. And all because you bought, and read, and REALLY DO the things that Dom tells you in *Walk Yourself Wealthy*.

Of course, YOU don't HAVE to buy Dom's book. You could just let Tom, Dick and Harry buy it instead. And in a year or two you can be thinking 'Yeah, I used to have a dog walking business that I really loved.' Of course, by then you'll probably be working for Tom, Dick or Harry.

Ouch.

There are also strategies and advice in his book that cost a FORTUNE to get hold of. I know because I have spent a fortune getting them myself. Frankly, I wish he hadn't put them in, but that's Dom for you.

Dom doesn't just talk the talk like all the others. He really walks the walk. He is genuine. A huge amount of what he says is as the result of the knowledge of hard-won experience. He's been where you are now. He also knows how to get YOU where he is now.

He means this stuff. He does this stuff.

So should you.

Fetch!"

Nick Holmes – Scrum Master
www.nickhewynholmes.co.uk

"Having already been impressed with *How To Be Your Dog's Superhero*, I knew Dominic's second book would entertain, offer something a little bit different, and most importantly be packed full of useful, actionable information.

I was not disappointed! Dom covers the big, essential concepts any pet business owner needs to grasp in order to stand out in today's market.

The length of this book is inversely disproportionate to its value; it's a short read, but if you take Dom's advice and put his tried-and-tested methods into action, you'll transform

your business."
Alex Wardle – Artifact Media
www.artifactmedia.co.uk

"Everything Dom writes about in this book is spot on. Although I have a dog, and she does like a walk or three, I'm not in the dog walking business. I have a wholesale coffee company but all the principles outlined in this book are valid for any type of business, and what's more they work, when implemented.

My customers are coffee shops, restaurants, etc. most of whom wait to see who walks through the door. Those that apply premium positioning, premium pricing and the other marketing foundations that Dom talks about in this book are the ones that are growing fast.

In fact, my busiest customers are the ones that charge the most for their products!

Funny that!"
Chris Hamlett – The Coffee Baron
www.flyingcoffee.co.uk

Contents

INTRODUCTION

Congratulations on buying this book and welcome to my world. You've taken the first, vital step towards transforming your dog walking business.

I wrote *Walk Yourself Wealthy* to help dog walkers who want to take their passion for working with dogs and turn it into a money-making machine.

Wealthy though? Is it really possible to get wealthy from dog walking?

Well, not without lots of hard work, that's for sure. But yes, it is possible for you to create a very profitable business that provides you with an excellent income and enough money for continued investment in your business, time off, holidays and nice things for your family.

And unlike most of the bullshit pet business marketing books out there, this one has been written by someone who has implemented all of the marketing secrets in his own dog adventure business too. Namely, me!

Yes indeed. I started my very own premium dog adventure company in the middle of a recession in my own home town of Sunderland (in a less than salubrious part of North East England). I will go more into my own story a little later, but don't think for one minute you can't apply these strategies and turn your business from ordinary to amazing too.

This short book will give the marketing tools you need to elevate your business from being seen as just another dog walker to be recognised as the premium dog walking business in your town. And the only choice for the most discerning clients who want a personal high-end service and are prepared to pay a fair whack to get it.

Why you need to be different

The pet industry is booming and this is especially true of the dog sector. This is obviously great news for anyone with a dog walking business. Despite being busier than ever, most people see dog ownership as a box they must tick to complete their family. People want to own a dog, but they need help looking after their dog (or dogs).

Add to the mix an almost unlimited number of products and services that dog owners can 'baby-fy' their dogs with (in a similar way to which we spoil our children), and you have a thriving industry that is virtually recession-proof.

When an industry is growing strongly, much like the dog walking sector is now, it's easy for almost any new starter business to pick up at least a few clients. But, as more people see the opportunity and take up dog walking as a profession, it becomes harder to stand out from the crowd. You may have noticed his happening in your town already, with increased competition springing up every other week.

That's business I'm afraid. It's tough and unforgiving, and in any industry with fierce competition, there will be winners and losers. As the market becomes more saturated, it will be the business owners who know how to market effectively who will attract the best clients, stay in business longer and, ulti-mately, be the most successful.

In my capacity as a pet business coach, I've worked with many dog walking businesses, and I've found that no matter how long you have been in business or where your business is located, the chances are there are usually lots of simple improvements you can make to your marketing that will dramatically improve your positioning and boost your profits.

The problem when you are so involved in the day-to-day running of your business is you rarely have time to think about marketing and plan how you can improve things.

This book will change all that, but before we dive into the training, maybe it's time I introduced myself properly.

I'm Dom Hodgson, the founder of the UK's number-one dog adventure company, Pack Leader Dog Adventures. I'm also the author of numerous dog training and pet business books, and I regularly consult with pet businesses all over the world, helping them to improve their marketing so they can substantially grow their profits.

In *Walk Yourself Wealthy* I will be sharing with you five simple but extremely powerful marketing secrets that any business can do, but almost no one ever does. These strategies will help you control how people think about your business so you can attract great clients who are prepared to pay good money for the excellent services you offer.

That said, none of that will happen unless you have the balls (or the ladyballs) to implement what I teach you in the book.

There's no fluff or flannel and definitely no woo woo 'manifest yourself a million dollars' bullshit in this book. Despite what the unicorn-believing mindset gurus will tell you, you can't just wish your way to a better business. It takes real action and a plan to follow.

Well, this is that plan. You provide the action.

Are you striving to be five star?

You will hear me mentioning the benefits of being 'premium' a lot in this book, and that is quite deliberate.

It's much easier for your business to thrive and make healthy profits if you are positioned at the top end of the market. If you can market to the more affluent clientele who have the money and the wherewithal to spend it, you can make more money faster and do less work than you would serving the bottom end of the market. This is true in any industry.

Higher-end clients recognise high-quality and amazing service and so are much less likely to move to a competitor just because they are cheaper. So it makes perfect sense for you to go for the meatiest slice of the pie and target those prospects who want the very best service for their dog and are prepared to pay handsomely for it.

Then you can let your competitors deal with the bargain hunters at the bottom end of the market.

The profit is in the positioning

You hopefully know what profit is, but what do I mean by positioning your business?

Well, positioning, to go by the dictionary description, is:

"A marketing strategy that aims to make a brand occupy a distinct position, relative to competing brands, in the mind of the customer." (Business Dictionary)

It's what you do in your marketing that affects how your prospective clients think of your dog walking business, compared to all the other dog walking businesses out there.

So, now it's time for me to ask:

What do people in your town really think of your dog walking business?

Do they feel lucky to even get an appointment with you, always pay on time and speak about your service to others like you are a celebrity dog walker?

Do they think you are the Rolls-Royce or the Fiat of the dog walking world?

Are you expensive and exclusive, or do you give great service at a fair price?

Or, are you (God forbid) cheap and cheerful?

The answers to these questions matter, a lot.

Bottom-feeding clients frequently cancel walks and expect you to fit them in at a moment's notice. They don't use you regularly enough and will generally treat your walking service as a grudge purchase they 'have' to make just because their dog needs a walk while they are at work.

Premium clients will regard your dog walking service as a vital, exclusive and frequent exercise ritual they 'must have' each and every week.

I hope you can see which of these groups you should be targeting.

Unfortunately, most of the dog walkers I speak to fall into the first category. They may have some great clients but would like more, and they know their service is worth more than what they are currently charging.

If that sounds like you, then don't panic, because the simple marketing secrets that I will share with you in this book will (if you implement them) allow you to be seen as the go-to, must-have, much-imitated-but-never-matched dog walking superstar in your town.

With great positioning comes great commitment

Some of the strategies in this book require a bit of work and patience, but many of them you can implement straight away and see an increase in your profits almost overnight.

Of course, that's just if you want more profit from your business.

If you are happy serving the bottom end of the market and eating beans every night, then this book definitely is not for you. You should send it back and I will gladly give you a refund.

This book also isn't for those who are content to bumble along with the same shitty clients who seem to want everything for nothing and constantly grumble about the prices you charge. Nor is it for those who treat their dog walking business like a vocational choice or a hobby business.

Not treating your dog business like a proper business is the fastest way to go out of business.

Who this book is for

This book is for dog walkers or those thinking of starting a dog walking business who want their business to provide a great income. It's for ambitious go-getters who have worked hard to become great at dog walking, know they offer an exceptional service and now they want the world to know it.

And it's OK to have a business that helps people AND makes money.

But there's a big difference between being great at what you do and being known as the best.

And despite what you may have been led to believe, it's not enough to simply be a good or even a great dog walker.

Of course, you have to be of a reasonable standard, and I'm assuming you already walk dogs to a very high standard. That alone, however, won't ensure you make the most money from your business.

The dog walkers who have the most successful businesses are the ones who are known for being the best dog walkers. You can be the most talented dog handler in the world, but if no one knows you are, then it's not so much of a plus. It's your reputation and what prospective clients believe about you which will determine how you are thought of in the market-place.

Being 'the best' means different things to different people and, despite what your family and friends might tell you, it really isn't enough anymore to offer a 'great, friendly service at a fair price'.

Let's get real.

A great, friendly service is the absolute bare minimum your clients are expecting. They want to be wowed and feel like they are receiving an exclusive service. And as more competition springs up like weeds in a flower bed, you will need to wow them (and keep wowing them) if you want to climb to the top of the mountain (and stay there).

The great news is that the more discerning prospects, especially those who want a lot more for their money than just a great, friendly service, are already out there. They are waiting for someone to fit the high standards they have set in their mind. And they are more than willing to pay more for something 'extra special'.

You just need to find them and convince them that yours is the business they should choose.

So how do you do that?

By marketing better than anyone else, of course. This is easier said than done. Elevating your business so you appear different and better than all the other dog walkers in town is a trick that only the most savvy business owners manage to pull off.

Will you be one of the lucky ones?

A word of warning before we begin. You will feel a lot of resistance to doing a lot of what I share with you over the next 60 pages. That's natural, and a lot of my business coaching clients feel the same way when I first begin to work with them.

But the very fact that you feel uncomfortable about it is a sure sign that you know it's the right thing to do, and any internal fear you feel is just because you are coming up against a new idea which goes against much of what you have been taught in the past.

"But my business is different!"

I hear this a lot, and I'm sorry, snowflake, but it really isn't. These marketing secrets have been tried and tested by thousands of different business in all kinds of niches, so don't think your business is particularly special and so different that they won't work for you.

Business is business the world over, and people always buy the things they want. You just need to make sure that your business is the one they want to buy from.

I will round off this introduction by stressing again that this isn't a theory book. Everything I talk about I have implemented in my own dog adventure business, and I know you will have great success if you employ these strategies in your dog business.

So without further ado, let's dive in with one of the most simple-to-implement positioning and marketing secrets there is: premium pricing.

CHAPTER 1

BE PREMIUM

"Price is what you pay. Value is what you get"
Warren Buffett

Here's a question for you.

Which do you think is easier to sell: one new £264,000 Rolls-Royce Dawn or 26 Ford Fiestas?

You guessed it; it's the Rolls-Royce Dawn.

Why?

Well, it's all to do with who you are targeting the sale at.

So for sure you would struggle (and very likely fail) to sell a Rolls-Royce to someone looking for a Ford Fiesta, but if you targeted your advert at the CEO of a FTSE 100 company, a Premier League footballer or a Saudi prince, it would probably be quite an easy sale. In fact, the problem may be would the Rolls-Royce be exclusive enough for the buyer.

So if you get your targeting right, then yes, selling one Rolls-Royce should be far easier than selling 26 Ford Fiestas.

Selling even one of the 26 Fords is made even more difficult because in that price range there is a huge choice of similar-looking vehicles. Volkswagen, SEAT, Vauxhall and ŠKODA all offer a similar kind of thing at a very similar price. This is

11

one reason why you see so many car dealers run discounted price promotions, all the time. When there is little to separate similar-looking cars, price becomes the only point of difference.

This works with every kind of product and service. Including dog walking.

Where does your dog walking business sit when compared to all the other people offering a similar kind of service in your town?

This is important because generally we are prepared to pay more for something if we perceive it to be better quality.

Why pricing matters

You wouldn't go to Harrods and expect to purchase the same items at the same price as you would in Aldi or another discount store.

But is Harrods a better store because its products are five times better, or is it perceived to sell better products because it charges five times the price?

Well, it's a weird quirk of pricing, but many consumers will infer that a product or service is better quality than a lower-priced one simply because it's more expensive.

You can use this to your advantage and immediately position your services as better and more desirable than all the rest, simply by making your dog walking service the most expensive in your town.

Ah, but you have competition and couldn't possibly charge any more than you do, right?

Wrong, and I will explain why.

Let's move away from the Harrods and Rolls-Royces and take a closer look at the town you live in.

Look around your town the next time you go for a walk or are driving to work. Have a look at the different cars people are driving, the Fords and Ferraris. See the different houses for sale, cheap flats and council houses and huge private gated mansions. Now think about all of the bars, restaurants and shops in your town centre. Do they offer the same products at the same price in exactly the same way?

The answer is no, they don't.

In every town and city all over the world, there are expensive and cheaper choices for every product or service you can think of. If you look hard enough, you will find both a high-end luxury and a bargain-basement option.

So if you are such a great dog walker, then it begs the question, why aren't you charging the highest prices?

Premium pricing is the most easy-to-implement marketing secret and, as scary as it may seem, pricing your dog walking service at the very top end of the market will immediately position you among the best, if not as 'the best' dog walker in your town.

I mean, you must be the best. You are the most expensive, right?

That's certainly what the more affluent prospects in your area will be thinking. They are used to paying more for the best clothes, food and other services they buy, so there's no reason to doubt they will pay more for the best dog walker for their beloved dog.

As Dan Kennedy says in his excellent book *No B.S. Marketing To The Affluent*, "It takes no more work to attract customers from the explosively growing affluent population who are eager to pay premium prices in return for exceptional expertise, service and experiences."

If it takes no more work, then it really comes down to choice and whether you have the cajones to go after the high end of the market.

And it's not just the affluent who will be eager to get their hands on your exclusive dog walking service.

Most of us aspire to have better things, and we buy the best we can afford whenever we can. Dog owners are no exception. I know many dog owners who will gladly eat spam sandwiches or beans on toast while their dog will be chomping on organic duck breast and blueberries for tea. So while being premium priced means you will attract more affluent dog owners, there are many other dog owners who will find money in their budget because they want the very best for their dog too.

Of course, this premium pricing tactic is much easier to implement if you are excellent at what you do (and you will soon be found out if you aren't very good). But I'm guessing you are already pretty good at walking dogs...

"But I need more experience!" I hear you cry.

You do not. As Stephen Covey, author of *The 7 Habits Of Highly Effective People*, said, "Experience is very overrated", and I tend to agree with him.

The biggest mistake you can make as a new dog walking business owner is to assume that you can't position your new business at the top end of the market because you don't have the same experience as X, or your grooming parlour isn't as fancy as Y. Yes, you need to be of a certain standard, but the whole 'more experience deserves more money' thing is a big pile of horseshit.

If you believe your competitors who have been dog walking for ten years are ten years better than you, then surely they will always be ten years better than you, and you might as well just give up now.

Ah, but putting your prices up will mean you lose clients, right?

Wrong again.

You may lose a few, but they will likely be the PITA (Pain in the Arse) clients that cause you hassle and you wanted rid of anyway.

To build a business you love working in and enjoy making money from will mean you don't serve everyone.

Cheap ain't cheerful

It might be cheerful for the customer, but the type of customers you attract when you are cheap are usually bargain-hunting bottom feeders who complain about the price, never pay on time and cancel appointments when they find someone who is cheaper than you.

Let's go back to the point I made at the start of this chapter. Do you think it's easier to serve one client who pays £30 for a dog walk, or two who pay £15, or three who pay £10?

Obviously it's the one who pays the most. When you are a premium-priced business, you actually need fewer clients, which means you can give them an enhanced service and much more attention.

I know; it's a scary thought to put your prices up.

What if clients leave, or what if they stop coming through the door? Well, these things almost never happen, and the increased profits more than make up for any clients you lose (who are usually the bottom-feeding cheapskates we mentioned earlier).

So yeah, it may be scary, but that's no reason not to do it, and the fact is that premium pricing is the fastest and easiest marketing secret you can implement. You can do it today.

Right now.
So do it!

Premium pricing bonus

Premium pricing is one of the first things I teach my apprentices inside my 'Pet Business Inner Circle', and I know you will feel a lot of resistance to putting up your prices. But put them up you must, and to help you I am giving you access to a Premium Pricing Video Masterclass that I did for them. You can get free access to this exclusive training by going to www.growyourpetbusinessfast.com and clicking on the free resources tab.

Action point

Start today by committing to becoming the top dog walker in your town, and put your prices up now, by at least 10%.

Remember, you won't be considered the best in town unless you charge the best prices. And best, in this case, means the highest.

Don't let a lack of experience stop you from vaulting over the competition and claiming the mantle of most expensive (and therefore the most desirable) dog walker in your town. If you are good at what you do, then you deserve to be paid the best price possible, and if you don't think your service deserves to be paid the most money, then you should probably question whether you should be offering that service at all.

There are many ways to justify to your prospects why they should pay your higher prices, and I go into one of the easiest ways to do that in chapter 2.

CHAPTER 2

BE SPECIALISED

"If you don't specialise, you ain't that special"
Dom Hodgson

Where in the world will you find the best Irish coffee?

Dublin? Cork? County Down?

Wrong!

It's San Francisco, of course.

This story was first relayed to me by my friend Chris 'The Coffee Baron' Hamlett, who helps coffee shop owners grow their profits, and the following copy comes straight from the Buena Vista Cafe's website.

The historic venture started on the night of November the 10th in 1952. Jack Koeppler, then-owner of the Buena Vista, challenged international travel writer Stanton Delaplane to help re-create a highly touted "Irish Coffee" served at Shannon Airport in Ireland. Intrigued, Stan accepted Jack's invitation, and the pair began to experiment immediately.

Throughout the night the two of them stirred and sipped judiciously and eventually acknowledged two recurring problems. The taste was "not quite right," and the cream would not float. Stan's hopes sank like the cream, but Jack was undaunted. The restau-

19

rateur pursued the elusive elixir with religious fervour, even making a pilgrimage overseas to Shannon Airport.

Upon Jack's return, the experimentation continued. Finally, the perfect-tasting Irish whiskey was selected. Then the problem of the bottom-bent cream was taken to San Francisco's mayor, a prominent dairy owner. It was discovered that when the cream was aged for 48 hours and frothed to a precise consistency, it would float as delicately as a swan on the surface of Jack's and Stan's special nectar.

Success was theirs! With the recipe now mastered, a sparkling clear, six-ounce, heat-treated goblet was chosen as a suitable chalice.

Soon the fame of the Buena Vista's Irish coffee spread throughout the land. Today, it's still the same delicious mixture, and it's still the same clamorous, cosmopolitan Buena Vista.

Have you ever read such a compelling description of a coffee shop? I'm guessing not. The owners of the Buena Vista Cafe know how powerful it is to put a great core story at the heart of your marketing.

They also understand the power of finding and owning a niche.

And niches don't get much more obscure than serving the best Irish coffee, right in the heart of San Francisco.

This is a big business too. The Buena Vista Cafe sell over 2,000 Irish coffees a day.

Yowsers.

That's not all, because they also sell a shitload of other coffees, teas and biscuits as well as breakfasts, dinners and desserts (bread-and-butter pudding with Irish whiskey anyone? Mmm). And they even have a gift shop where you can buy T-shirts, caps and all kinds of other useless (but highly profitable) merchandise.

But in spite of all the other things they sell, they are known for their Irish coffee.

So what does a coffee seller halfway around the world have to do with you?

Well, finding and owning a niche is one of the easiest ways to stand out from your competitors and position you as an industry expert.

You just need to decide what to niche down to, in your business.

What's your niche?

Could you walk only small dogs?

Big dogs?

Gun dogs?

Just cocker spaniels?

How does the thought of only walking one kind of dog make you feel?

Terrified, I bet.

You couldn't possible specialise like that, could you?

Well yes, you can. Niching down and specialising is one of the easiest ways to position yourself as an expert.

Yes, it's scary to niche down. You think by narrowing down your market you are cutting off lots of potential clients, and in some ways you are. But remember the Buena Vista Cafe. Even though they sell 2,000 Irish coffees every day, they still sell a lot of other things too.

Niching down allows you to stand out and attract the people who will be interested in your specialised service.

Here's an example.

Let's imagine I am a responsible dog owner who has just acquired a little cocker spaniel, and I am looking for a dog walker to help me out.

So I look through the Yellow Pages or Google, and despite the fact there are lots of dog walkers in my town, the choice is surprisingly easy. One business shines out like a beacon to me.

I can either choose one of the regular run-of-the-mill dog walkers (who offer very similar services which vary a little in price, but not by much), or I can choose Karen's Cocker Club, where one of Karen's Cocker Crew picks up all the cocker spaniels she walks in the Cockermobile and takes them on a breed-specific adventure where they can practise gun dog games that are perfectly suited to match a cocker spaniel's character.

Well, if I love my cocker (and I do love my cocker dearly), and I care deeply about the type of care he gets, then obviously I'm going to pick the specialist operation. Not only that, but I will also be prepared to pay more for such an exclusive and bespoke service. This leads nicely on to the other main reason you should consider niching in your dog walking business.

There's riches in niches

Niching down and specialising allows you to charge much more for your services which, by their specialist nature, are more personal and exclusive. Also, catering for only one or two breeds like this makes it much easier for you to offer additional products and services that are specific to your target market, and not worry about carrying loads of stock to cater for every breed.

It's way easier to stand out from the crowd when you own a niche too.

While everyone else is offering 'great service at a fair price', you are offering 'specialist cocker spaniel adventures', and this gives you a USP that no one else has. You could take it even further and give yourself a title like the 'Queen of Cockers'.

Enough about cockers though. There are many other options for you to ponder.

For example, you could choose a specific size of dog or even a type of dog, like gun dogs or herders or maybe all dogs under knee height. Maybe your niche isn't about the type of dog but instead the experience you offer.

I did this with my own dog walking business.

When everyone else was offering 15-, 30-, 45- and 60-minute walks, I just offered one option, a 1.5-hour adventure, and I charged a premium for it too. I aimed the service at gun dog and working dog owners, expecting just cocker spaniel, Labrador and pointer owners to want the service.

Well, I did get some gun dogs, but I also got pugs, Samoyeds and French bulldogs. All because they wanted an 'adventure' for their dogs. The adventure was the thing that sold it.

Some things to consider before you niche.

Obviously, when you niche down to a breed, you want to make sure there are enough dogs for you to walk. It's no good marketing yourself as King of Afghan Adventures if there are only two Afghan hounds in your whole town. But it shouldn't be hard to research what the most popular breeds of dog are where you live, or if you already own a walking business, just look at your current client list and see what numbers you have of each dog.

Is there a breed category in your town that you can serve with a specialised service, and that you enjoy walking? Well, that could be the niche for you.

So that's marketing secret number 2 – Be Specialised. And if specialising has whet your appetite, then you will love marketing secret number 3 – Be the Expert, because the next chapter is all about taking you from a mere mortal dog walker to someone who is revered as the fount of all dog walking knowledge within your industry.

Action point

Without a doubt, niching is almost as scary as premium pricing but, as before, just because it's scary doesn't mean you shouldn't do it.

Start researching now what you can niche down to and then proclaim yourself queen of the 'whatevers'. With some thought, you can build all your marketing around your new niche. If it is crystal clear to your prospects about exactly what your niche is on your website, leaflets, social media and other marketing materials, then in no time at all you will apportion a huge slice of the market all for yourself as the self-anointed expert in that niche.

CHAPTER 3

BE THE EXPERT

"Who's to say who's an expert?"
Paul Newman

A giant ship's engine failed. The ship's owners tried one expert after another, but no one could figure out how to fix the engine.

Then they brought in an old man who had been fixing ships since he was young. He carried a large bag of tools with him, and when he arrived, he immediately went to work. He inspected the engine very carefully, top to bottom.

Two of the ship's owners were there, watching this man, hoping he would know what to do. After looking things over, the old man reached into his bag and pulled out a small hammer. He gently tapped something. Instantly, the engine lurched into life. He carefully put his hammer away. The engine was fixed!

A week later, the owners received a bill from the old man for 10,000 dollars.

"What?!" the owners of the ship exclaimed. "He hardly did anything!"

So they wrote the old man a note saying, "Please send us an itemised bill."

The man sent a bill that read:

Tapping with a hammer........................ $ 1.00

Knowing where to tap.......................... $ 9,999.00

That's a much-told but very cool story which demonstrates quite nicely how you can charge almost anything you want, when you are considered the expert.

Why experts are special

Experts are considered the leaders in their field. Their opinions are sought after and written about, and their time is considered more valuable than that of just a run-of-the-mill practitioner.

Their fees are generally a lot higher than non-experts too, and that is one of the main reasons you need to acquire expert status.

Experts get paid more money.

Fact.

But how do you become an expert?

Well, if you have trained to become a dog walker for a long time, then you will already have a certain level of expertise. So maybe the question should be:

How do you become known as an expert?

Once again, I should stress that you will quickly get found out if you just pretend to be an expert at anything you aren't. So if you aren't an expert, then first work hard at getting good at doing 'the thing', in this case, dog walking.

If you need more help with the dog behaviour side of your business, then you should get a copy of my bestselling dog training book *How To Be Your Dog's Superhero* from www.mydogssuperhero.com

Then, once you are great at walking, it's time to turn your efforts to telling the world how good you really are, so they see you as an expert.

And I'm not recommending you stand on a park bench shouting "I AM THE EXPERT. LISTEN TO ME!" at everyone who passes by with a dog.

There are much easier ways to cement your expert status in the eyes of your target market.

Make no mistake though; your reputation and how well known you are for being a great dog walker is a huge factor in determining how much demand there will be for your dog walking services, and how much you can charge for them.

It's certainly a bigger factor than how good you are at dog walking.

Why it's not about that 'thang' you do

Think of a three-Michelin-starred chef whose restaurant is sold out months in advance. Yes, the three stars prove he is a masterchef and can cleverly balance perfectly cooked potatoes, mushrooms and chicken on top of fancy pea puree. But, it's his reputation, including his TV appearances, magazine articles and the books he has written which cement his expert status in the public's mind.

So can you pinch some expert marketing secrets of the rich and famous to show the prospective clients in your town that you are the wise and trusted expert?

Absolutely you can, and one of the best ways to catapult yourself above your competition is to do what all famous people do, and that is write a book.

The power of a book

The 2007 line-up of US presidential candidates was a mish-mash of senators, governors, former big-city mayors and a retired four-star army general. However, they all had one thing in common.

They had all written a book.

And most of them had written a book as a tool to help tell their story as they launched their bid for the presidency.

Mark Halperin, the political director of ABC News, said at the time: "You're not a real candidate, Pinocchio, if you haven't written your own book."

I would take this a step further and say you aren't considered a real expert until you have written a book. That's easy for me to say, of course, because I've written one.

Writing a book might seem a bit overkill in the quest for expert status, but don't write it off as something that 'other people do'. Using a book you have written as a powerful marketing tool applies as much to you and your dog walking business as it does to those seeking to become President of the United States.

Let's clarify a few things though. We aren't talking about you writing a book in order to become a bestselling author. That would be nice, but it's highly unlikely to happen.

Your book is there to do a different job. It's there to position you as the expert dog walker in your town, county or even the country.

The dog walker who is the author of *Five Essential Questions You Need To Ask A Dog Walker* or *How To Enjoy Stress-Free Walks With Your Dog* is going to stand out like a sore thumb from the rest of the average competition in that town.

A published book (even a self-published book) is a powerful marketing tool, and saying you are a published author will immediately elevate you into the realms of experthood.

Why?

Well, very few people even read many books these days, and far fewer actually write them. Jaws drop and people look at you like you are some kind of superhuman when you tell them you are a published author.

If you market it correctly, then you and your book will also get publicity which will further cement your expert status, not to mention get you leads you can turn into clients.

This isn't the easiest positioning task to accomplish, and you will need to set aside time each day to write it, but, in my experience, writing a book is the single most important thing you can do to improve your positioning if you are serious about growing your business.

And I practise what I preach too. My first bestselling dog training book helped position me as an expert in my field. It has spent time at the top of the Amazon Dog Care chart as well as help many thousands of dog owners around the world who have bought and read it. You never know, you may get a taste for writing too.

I certainly did.

As well as *How To Be Your Dog's Superhero*, I have repurposed this book *Walk Yourself Wealthy* into two other books as well, and I have a more comprehensive pet business book *Grow Your Pet Business FAST!* out very soon, as well as some other projects I am collaborating with other expert authors on.

Mine are all instructional books to one degree or another, but they also have a lot of my personality in them, and that's a key point.

Your book, if you write it correctly, can be the perfect ice-breaker for your prospects to learn more about you and your business. That's because as well as all the expert enhancing benefits writing a book bestows upon you, it also enables you to tell your story and within that story share your beliefs, values and passions.

It's a cheesy and oft-trotted-out line, but people really do buy people. So if you do write a book, then make sure that it has lots of your personality in it. That will enable people to feel like they know more about you and your values as well as your services, before they even enquire about your dog walking service.

So how do you put your personality into it?

Well, alongside the dog care tips you share, you can also tell stories about your life as a dog walker. Any silly incident that happens on a walk has the potential to be turned into a story.

My friend Kat Smith, who helps salon owners grow their businesses, helped to write a book called *101 Naked Confessions Of A Gay Hairdresser* based on the stories of her then business partner Terry. This book was essentially repurposed emails about funny stories from the salon that Kat had written. Then she topped and tailed them and included a few hairdressing tips.

The book was a massive success for Kat and Terry and helped them grow their salon business immensely. Could a book about dog walking do the same thing for your business too?

The ultimate marketing tool

Having a book makes it very easy to market your business. Essentially, your book sells your business and you sell the book.

Easy, eh?

Course it is. Now you just need to write one.

There isn't room here to go into the details of how to write one; just take my word for it that you need to write a book. Yes, it will take time, but it is worth it. Trust me.

Book writing bonus

To help inspire you to move forward and actually write a book, I have some more in-depth training you can access. 'Why your book is the best business card' is a one-hour audio training I recorded with my friend Vicky Fraser. Vicky is a copywriter, book coach and small business ass-kicker, and I published my first book in 90 days using her online course. This audio training will give you a much more detailed overview of how and why you should write a book to grow your dog walking business. Go to www.growyourpetbusinessfast.com and click on the free resources tab to access the training.

In the meantime, here are some other things you can do to quickly cement your expert status.

Publicity

Publicity is something that, with a bit of persistence, any dog walking business can get. Obviously there's your book, which you will publicise like crazy once you have written it, but what else can you get publicity for?

Well, books aren't the only places you will find shaggy dog stories.

Spend five minutes browsing through your local rag, and you will inevitably find a dog story. I've never failed to find at least two dog-related stories in every edition of every paper I've ever read. This is especially true of my local paper.

People love dogs

No shit, Sherlock. They really do. They love pictures of them and they love reading about them. And they also love reading about people who do nice things for dogs and who work with dogs, and weird quirky dog business stories too.

So get your thinking cap on and come up with some news-worthy story that will interest your paper. The business section editor may be interested in the niche that you are specialising in or even feature you in a new-business article if you have just started trading. Then there are charity events, sponsored walks and all kinds of things you can pique a journalist's interest with.

You need to be persistent, and don't expect it to happen straight away, but once you get a break, then make sure they mention your contact details in the article, which most reporters will do anyway. This exposure may directly bring you some new clients, but that's not the main reason to do it.

Why you need to get your picture in the paper

This might sound vain and pathetic but it's entirely true. People are impressed if you have been in the paper (providing it's not the court round-up, of course). And proclaiming "As seen in the Waterford Post" on your website and other marketing materials is as impressive (if not more impressive) to your prospects then any certifications on your about page or letters you have after your name.

Publicity isn't limited to newspapers either. You can submit stories for use on the radio and in dog magazines. These media outlets are always looking for good content they can push out to their audience. The first rule of any kind of marketing is don't be boring, so give your stories a twist that makes them irresistible to hungry journalists.

Expert status is something every dog walker should aim for, and the strategies I have outlined here will help get you started. Don't make the mistake of thinking you are too small a fish or that you have nothing to say that hasn't been said already. That kind of thinking will keep you being that small fish.

Becoming known as the best in your town is much easier than being best in the world, and it won't take much to elevate your business and make it stand out from all the average competition. Once you have done that, you will dominate your local area.

The next marketing secret I am sharing with you will help pull towards you the kind of clients you really want to work with. It will turn you into a magnet for great clients and also repel the type of clients who aren't a good fit for you and your business.

Action point

There are two action points in this chapter. One is quick and easy, and the other will take a bit more time but is crucial to your long-term success.

---

1. Get in the paper. I'm not suggesting you rob a bank or steal a car. All publicity is not good publicity. But it shouldn't be too hard for you to get your dog walking business in your local (and maybe a national) paper. It could even be as simple as sending a press release about your business. Chances are you will have to be a bit more creative though, so buy a few copies of your local paper and check out the type of dog stories they are writing about regularly. These are the stories that people are obviously reading, so if you can put a twist on one of those, then you are halfway there. Then be persistent (but not a dick). Follow up with the journalist and send the press release out a few times to a few different journalists. If your story is interesting enough, then eventually someone will bite.

2. Write your book. I know, I know, you can't write a book; you simply don't have the time or anything to write about. Wrong, mon ami, you need to make time for this, and if you are great at what you do (and you want to be considered an expert), then you should have no problem talking passionately about your expert subject, which is essentially what you will be doing in your book.

    Remember, it's not about how big it is – it's what you do with it that matters (oo err missus). Seriously, think of your book as a short guide that will help your prospects solve a small part of a problem. You will find once you start writing that it will probably expand and you will want to include many other topics. Getting started is the key though. Don't wait for the muse to land on your shoulder and grant you inspiration, or you will be waiting a very long time.

Demonstrating your expertise is the main driver behind writing your book and getting your name (and face) in the paper. The expertise and celebrity factor will help position you as being different to every other dog walker out there. And being different is what the next chapter is all about, so let's crack on to marketing secret number 4, Be Polarising.

CHAPTER 4

BE POLARISING

"I don't set out to offend or shock, but I also don't do anything to avoid it"

Sarah Silverman

As a small business, one of the most potent marketing weapons you have is your personality. If you can put your personality into your marketing, you will quickly build a tribe of people who are just like you.

The problem is most business owners either don't have a personality or they are afraid to use it.

This is a big mistake.

The businesses that are most successful are the ones that have a unique identity and stand out from the competition. But to stand out you need to stand for something, and if you don't stand for anything then you won't stand out at all.

Standing out doesn't mean having a fancy logo or even a cool and quirky business name. The advertising strategies that big brands like Coca-Cola, Mastercard and Asda use aren't much use in your business. I'm talking about putting more of your beliefs, opinions and personality into your marketing.

Don't for a minute discount the lessons in this chapter. Putting more of 'you' into your marketing will help you pull your ideal client towards you AND make it easier for them to want to buy from you. Allow me to explain.

Before we buy anything from anyone, we generally go through a clearly defined process of:

- Know
- Like
- Trust

Your prospective clients have to get to know, like and trust you, *before* they buy from you.

Some clients, if they meet you face to face, will like and trust you almost immediately, but more often than not, this process takes a bit of time. This ties in with lead generation marketing which all dog walkers can and should do (but hardly anyone does). I will explain exactly how you can implement lead generation marketing in your business in the secret sixth chapter of this book...

Why does personality matter?

Think about your own buying experiences in the past. If you need some work doing in your house, unless it's an emergency and you need someone double quick to stop a leak, you rarely just phone up a random gas fitter, electrician or decorator, sign up for their service and pay the cash straight away.

You will first ask for a quote, and if they come round your house, you will try and suss them out a bit before you buy. Or you may ask a friend if they know anyone they can recommend because a recommendation from someone you know means they are more trustworthy.

Any business you can get from word of mouth is great, but you can't rely on just word of mouth.

So how do you get people to trust you enough to hand over money for your service even when they have never met you before?

By using your personality, of course.

Put more of 'you' into your business

By putting more of your personality into your marketing, you will attract people who share your values and believe in the same things you do. This makes them more likely to turn into paying clients, eventually.

It's a cheesy saying, but you need your prospects to buy into you before they buy from you. And it's a hell of a lot easier for them to know what it is they are buying into if you are open and honest about who you are and what you are about, in all your marketing literature.

By putting your personality front and centre, you make it very easy for people who share your values and believe in the same things as you to seek you out and want to use your services.

There's a big myth in business that you need to be 'professional' all the time. Sadly, most people mistake 'being professional' with 'being boring'.

I'm very professional with the service I deliver, but I'm not afraid to put my personality into everything I do because I know that it helps pull the right kind of clients towards me, and these are the people I want to work with.

41

Here's an example for you.

When I wrote my bestselling dog training book *How To Be Your Dog's Superhero*, I put all of my personality into the book. The terrible training mistakes I had made with my own dogs, swear words I use and also all of my beliefs about dog training. Like you shouldn't let your dog play with other dogs if you want him to stay near you when you exercise him off leash. This immediately made my book different to any of the 'politically correct', boring dog training books out there.

Not many fluffy-bunny dog trainers approved of it, many still don't, but I don't care because they aren't the ones paying me money. So by being polarising in my book, I pushed people away from me who were never going to buy my services anyway.

Being polarising like this also did something else.

It pulled towards me loads of dog owners who were suffering from the same problems as me. These people loved their dogs dearly, but they were frustrated as hell that their dogs wouldn't listen to them. These were real people who live, breathe, eat and take a shit the same way as I do. Which is the same way you do too, by the way…

The point is that me putting my beliefs and my personality front and centre in my business is one of the key reasons my business is so successful. I try to do this in all my marketing. My podcasts are opinionated and forthright, and my daily emails are the same. I do this for a reason. I don't want someone who might be considering hiring me to be shocked and appalled by the way I speak when they meet me.

And this isn't me putting on an act. How I'm speaking to you now in this book is how I would talk to you in person. When dog walkers attend my business talks, they say they feel like they already know me because they have built up a relationship and learned about my personality through my books, podcasts and daily emails.

I don't expect you to throw this book down and break into a chorus of 'I am what I am'. In fact, it may not suit you to be as forward in your business as I am in mine. But even if you don't want to put your whole self into your marketing, like I do, you should still put more of your opinions and beliefs into your marketing. For the simple reason that it will make it easier for you to attract the type of clients into your business that you really want to work with.

How to put yourself 'Out There'

Is there an issue that affects your prospects' dogs that they aren't aware of? Then talk about it in your marketing, and you will attract more of the clients who are suffering from that problem.

Is there something that other, less reputable dog walkers in your industry regularly do that you completely disagree with? Then make a point of telling your clients that you never do that.

This method of putting your personality into marketing works like gangbusters at repelling the clients that really aren't a good fit for you and would be better served going somewhere else.

43

I will say it again for those hard of reading. You can be professional without being boring, and you can use your personality to drive up your profits and enjoy yourself more, at the same time.

This type of teaching goes against what the average business owner will tell you, but maybe there's a reason they just have an average business.

Action point

Think of three things that you think make you different from every other dog walker in your town.

Now ask yourself why they make you different and why it will benefit a potential client to use your service over someone else's.

Then ask yourself why you do those things. What drives you to do them, what's your motivation? Is there a story behind why you do the things you do in your business?

That is the thing you need to be talking about in your marketing.

There's an excellent TED Talk by Simon Sinek called 'Start With Why' which you can watch on YouTube. Having a 'why' is important in how you inspire people to invest in your services.

Be honest and upfront about the reasons you do what you do, and don't be afraid to put more of your personality into all your marketing. It will transform your business.

CHAPTER 5

BE INACCESSIBLE

"It's a great feeling to be wanted but it's more exciting to be inaccessible"

Shreya Ghoshal

Have you ever flown first class across the Atlantic? Or sat in the house seats at the Royal Albert Hall? What about watched a concert in the 'VIP Golden Circle'?

No?

You need to get out more...

Imagine you are on holiday with your partner.

You head out for a meal together, but because you aren't familiar with the city you are staying in (and you didn't pack a guide book), you don't know where are the good places to eat.

Then you come across two restaurants side by side.

One is dark, dingy and dirty with two customers eating from a plate of plentiful but unappealing food, and the sign on the door says 'Happy Hour every hour'.

The next restaurant is heaving. The smell coming from inside is enticing and the buzz of activity is drawing you in. However, there is a small waiting area that is full of people and a sign hangs from the door which says '1 hour wait for a table'.

Which would you prefer to eat in?

Most people (myself included) would rather sample the food and atmosphere in the second restaurant.

If it's busy, it must be good, right?

The fact that there is a queue of people waiting only makes it seem more exclusive and desirable.

That is scarcity and exclusivity in action, and you can implement the same exclusivity in your own business too, which will make your services more desirable.

Here are a couple of things you can do to make your services appear more exclusive and desirable.

Have a signature service

Change your offering from just a dog walk to a specialised signature service.

When is a dog walk not a dog walk?

When it's 'Tammy's Gold Standard Terrier Trek', which includes:

- Breed-specific canine adventure
- Five-point health check
- Personalised play and train programme
- A happiness audit

- Daily socialisation checklist

And also comes with a fun-factor guarantee!

You get the idea, I hope. There really is no limit to the amount of extras you can bundle together into different combinations to make your service different to all the other standard 'dog walkers' out there. This brings me nicely on to tiered pricing options.

Many dog walkers make the mistake of having one standard walk which only varies in price based on the amount of time the dog is walked. This is a huge mistake and leaves a lot of potential money on the table. A better option is to have, well, more options.

So take the services I described above and bundle them into different price bands where the emphasis is on the experience the dog has and not the time he spends walking.

So you could have bronze, silver and gold star options for your walks with different extras added the more your clients pay.

Pricing your services like this will often lead to some clients upscaling to a better, more expensive service offering. It also makes lower-priced options seem more affordable in relation to a similar premium-priced option.

Another way to make your service seem more exclusive is make it more difficult for potential clients to get the chance to use your services.

So require them to fill in an application form and/or attend a pre-walk assessment before they are allowed to book an appointment to see you.

Having a barrier to entry like this will (much like the restaurant that makes you wait for an hour for a table) remove from the equation any time-wasting price shoppers who are 'just checking you out' and have no intention of using your service anyway. The people who do fill in the form and attend the assessment will put a greater value on your service because they have been made to jump through some hoops to get to you.

Clients who value things like high quality and exceptional service will break their necks to clamber over this 'velvet rope' you have placed around your business.

Making yourself less accessible to potential clients like this goes against a lot of the business advice you will get at your local networking group or Chamber of Commerce, but you shouldn't ignore it.

Having a small barrier to entry like this is crucial to you positioning yourself as an exceptional business and not like all the other normal pet businesses.

Action point

Think of a way you can package up your dog walking into a signature service that no other dog walker in your town, or even your county, is offering.

Once you do this, your business will appear unique to your prospects, and you will easily stand out from everyone else.

Because there is only one business offering your signature service (i.e. you!), then you can charge more for that service too. Your prospects can get any old dog walk from any dog walker, but they can only get 'Tammy's Terrier Treks' from you, and because there are only a limited number of spaces available each day, you can charge more for them.

Right, that's the five marketing secrets done with. Excited much?

You should be.

If you implement just one of these strategies, you will immediately elevate yourself above all the 'me too' pet businesses out there. If you have the courage to implement all five ideas, you will put your marketing on steroids and completely transform your business. I know. I've done it in my own business.

But you aren't finished yet.

Because in the secret sixth chapter I am going to share with you the very best way to plug all these marketing secrets into a marketing system that will ensure you have a queue of highly qualified clients who want to hire you.

Be warned though; there are no bright shiny objects in the secret sixth chapter. The lead generation marketing you will learn is only for serious pet business owners who are committed to learning tried-and-tested marketing methods that can work in any business.

So, if you are ready, turn the page and let's begin.

CHAPTER 6

THE SECRET SIXTH CHAPTER LEAD GENERATION MARKETING

You made it, well done!

Since you have arrived at the secret sixth chapter, I will assume you are committed to learning more about how to effectively market your amazing dog walking business.

Let's imagine you have launched a little dog walking business and you know there are dog owners in your town who need their dogs walking. You shouldn't need to convince them they need to find a walker for their dogs; they know that already, I hope. The marketing trick you need to pull off is to convince them to want to get their dogs walked by you.

And the easiest way to do that is with lead generation marketing. But before I introduce you to the wonderful world of lead generation marketing, it's probably a good idea for us to look at the wrong way that most pet businesses approach marketing.

How most 'normal' pet businesses work

Most businesses advertise their products or services by shouting very loudly about what they do (sometimes on flyers or in the local newspapers but more increasingly on social media). Then when they have shouted loud enough (usually about a special offer they are running), they may or may not get some people coming through the door, a small percentage of whom will go on to be clients.

But, and it's a big but, often these clients were only attracted by the initial offer. They are often (but not always) 'price buyers' and will jump ship and drop you like a used poo bag as soon as they see someone else offering the same thing as you, at a cheaper price.

These price buyers usually make terrible clients and are best avoided. Most of the other potential clients, who didn't buy from you, aren't even looking at the price you charge.

The fact is most people just don't buy straight away because they aren't ready to buy what you are selling, just yet.

They don't know you enough to trust you with their business.

There may be a few people who see your flyer or hear about you from a friend the very day they need a dog walker, but most of them simply won't need what you are offering, at the moment.

This doesn't mean to say they won't need you sometime in the future.

So they may have a dog, but they may not require a walker right now, or they may have a walker already they are happy with (but they may want to change in the future), or they may not even have a dog yet but are thinking about getting one in the future, and so may need a walker further down the line.

So there are a whole bunch of dog owners who could be potential clients of yours in the future, but you miss out on their business because they don't need you, yet.

But that's just business, right? You win some and you lose some.

Well, yes and no.

See, marketing in the style described above relies on the prospect buying your thing straight away.

So a prospect sees your leaflet or poster, or your advert on Facebook or in a magazine, or maybe they just stumble across your website. But before they get a chance to make a note of your contact details or bookmark your page, they get distracted. The phone rings or the dog barks, or they get a Facebook notification about their cousin's new hat, or they remember they have to go and pick the kids up from school. Then they are gone, and unless Mr or Mrs Dog Owner has a photographic memory, then you and your business are forgotten. Forever.

This style of marketing is known as 'off the page' selling. It relies on prospects buying straight away and is unfortunately how most businesses operate. They allow prospects to come and go, and there is rarely an attempt to take any details to follow up with the client, so the opportunity to make a sale is lost.

So wouldn't it be a great idea if we could somehow take that prospect's contact details and keep in touch with them over time, so that when they do need a dog walker, you are the first person they think of calling?

Well, there is, and it's called lead generation marketing.

The 'non-new' way to market your pet business

Firstly, I should stress there is nothing new about lead generation marketing. It has been around for many years, and you can apply the principles of it in almost any industry or business.

So what is it?

Lead generation is where, instead of allowing a prospect to leave your website (or your shop) straight away, you give them something in exchange for their contact details. Then you follow up with them relentlessly, both online and offline, and over time you position yourself as the obvious choice when they are actually ready to buy what it is you sell.

Here are two very good reasons why 'lead gen' is better than 'off the page' selling:

- Lead generation takes the pressure off you having to sell to someone straight away and allows you to keep in touch with them and so have many opportunities to sell to them, over time.
- Depending on the prospect (and how good your follow-up is), that 'keep in touch' phase may last a week, a month, six months or even a year or more. But in that time you can start to actually build a relationship with these prospects. You can bring them into your world, and by using the strategies we talked about earlier in the book, you will weed out the people who aren't a good fit for your service and pull towards you the perfect prospects so that, when they need a dog walker, you are the first person they think of.

Getting your prospects contact details so you can keep in touch and follow up with them sounds like an obvious (and a very profitable) thing to do, right?

Of course it does. So how do you do it?

Let's deal with each in turn.

How to get your prospects contact details

This is not as easy as you might think. Consumers are naturally protective of their contact details and reluctant to give them away, so we need to give them something in exchange. Ideally this will be something that is of high value to them but relatively inexpensive for us to produce and duplicate. The most commonly used thing is a free report or tip sheet. The king of direct response marketing Dan Kennedy named this a 'lead magnet'.

So, in your case, you could put together a short PDF that they can download for which the headline might be:

Five questions you must ask your potential dog walker

or

Discover the three crucial training mistakes that almost all irresponsible dog walkers make.

Your free report should be something that hits on a pain point and solves a problem your prospect has. Think of something that is causing them worry or frustration. And something that only your free report PDF will provide the answer to.

You aren't your prospect

You may have been dog walking for a number of years and know everything about the dog walking industry. Your prospect, however, does not. And if they are a dog owner who is looking for a dog walker (or will be sometime in the future), then downloading a free report that tells them the 'Five questions you must ask your potential dog walker' will be very useful indeed.

As an additional tip, the easiest way to find out what frustrations and worries your customers have is to just ask them in a survey or questionnaire. Don't think your clients don't have problems. We ALL have problems. Men, women, parents, golfers, horse and dog owners all have problems. You and I both have problems we need help fixing. The trick is to match the prospect's problem to your solution.

This is why targeting is so important.

I'm sure in the past you have been offered a free report or a tip sheet when you have landed on a website. That's lead generation in action. But I bet you only clicked on the advert and downloaded the PDF if you thought the free information would fix a problem you have. Well, the same rules apply to your prospects. You only want people expressing an interest and leaving their contact details if they have a problem your service can fix.

What happens next?

So the prospect gets their free report from you, which gives them the answer to the problem they have. The information you give should be easy for them to understand, and it should do what you promised it would, but no more than that. If you do that successfully, then your report will help to position you as an expert and a credible source of information, and it also allows you to tell a bit of your story too.

All of these elements are crucial to building the know, like and trust process that we know a prospect has to go through before they buy from us, which we talked about in chapter 4.

When do you start selling?

Well, that's up to you and there's no reason why you can't start selling to your prospects straight away, as soon as you have got their details. In fact, there may be some prospects who will convert into clients almost immediately. So you could include an offer at the end of the report for a free consult or phone call or a discounted service. But that will probably still be too soon for most people to consider jumping on board as a client. That's not a problem, though, because you have a secret weapon.

Their contact details. Specifically, their email address.

With their email address, you have the opportunity to do something which almost no other dog walking business will do, and that is follow up.

The fortune is in the follow-up

As I said before, even if you think you are 'the best dog walker in town', most prospective clients just aren't ready to buy at the first point of contact with you. But now you have their email address, you can follow up with them as many times as you like.

Emailing your clients is a very effective form of follow-up, and you can send daily, weekly or monthly emails. I send daily emails because I find the more emails I send, the more money I make.

To make email marketing work for you, the emails should be story-type emails rather than glossy newsletter brochure-type emails with pictures that you get from Next or Sports Direct.

Following up with email allows you to entertain and educate your prospect about what you do and how you can help them. And it gives you almost unlimited opportunities to remind them they can buy your service (also known as selling).

If you do that, then on the day they wake up and need a dog walker, you will be the first and only name that pops into their head.

Sending regular emails is only one way to follow up with your prospects, and it might not even be the most effective for you, so it's good to try a number of ways and see which one works best in your business. Whatever you do, though, don't dismiss email just because you don't like getting emails or think they won't work in your market. They will. I turned my business into the UK's number-one dog adventure company, launched two online businesses and have sold well over 1,000 copies of my books, all through email marketing.

Email Marketing Bonus

When I do my seminars and events, I always get questions about email marketing. So to help get you started I have a seven-day email crash course which shows you in more detail how you can use email marketing as the perfect follow-up to turn your prospects into clients and grow your dog walking business, fast! To get this course, go to www.growyourpetbusinessfast.com and click on the free resources tab.

Other ways to follow up with your potential clients

Offline follow-up can work wonders too, and by offline I mean anything that's not online, so phone calls, postcards, leaflets, newspaper adverts, etc.

Your book (which you are going to write, aren't you?) is a perfect introductory product which will give the client lots of useful information and help position you as the expert dog walker in your town (or the world). Nothing quite stamps your authority on a prospect's mind like your own book on a subject. It's the perfect business card and well worth spending time doing.

Your book is a great thing to sell in your emails too. Sales of your book may even help cover the cost of your advertising, as they have done for me in the past. It might even be worth you giving your book away to get your prospect's physical home address. Then you can follow up with them with the easiest follow-up tool, your monthly or quarterly newsletter.

Why you should have your own newsletter

A free, printed newsletter that you send out to your prospects every month or once a quarter is one of the best offline follow-up tools. You can get your prospects to sign up for the newsletter on the thank-you page after they have given the details for the free report, and you can keep offering it to them in your emails too.

The newsletter doesn't need to be anything fancy. A simple A4 piece of paper folded in half will be quite cheap to get printed up. In the newsletter you can include some dog walking tips, a bit of a story about something interesting that happened on a walk that month, maybe a recipe for some homemade dog biscuits and a customer of the month. Bingo. Easy peasy.

A physical newsletter like this is more powerful than just an email because it comes in the post, which almost forces your prospect to read it. It will also lie around their house for a week or so and act as a nice reminder to them that your business exists and it's where they should go when they need a dog walker.

Yes, all this follow-up is going to cost a certain amount of money, but it's much less than you think. And you need to stop thinking of this as a cost and instead think of it as investing in relationships with your clients.

Newsletter bonus

I practise what I preach and produce a free four-page monthly newsletter, 'The Pack Leader Business Gazette', for everyone who buys a copy of this book. In it, I tell stories and give business hints and tips, which helps me keep in touch with my tribe. To sign up for my free paper-and-ink newsletter, go to www.growyourpetbusinessfast.com and click the free resources tab.

Lifetime customer value

So you may spend £5, £10 or even £50 sending out a copy of your newsletter or book to a handful of prospects, but think of the return you will get back on that. If just one prospect out of ten turns into a client who then proceeds to get her dog walked once a week on your new gold package (£30), then it is more than worth the effort. (52 walks X £30 = £1,560 a year. Times that by three years or whatever is the average time a client uses your service, and you have £1,560 X 3 = £4,680.)

I think a £4,680 ROI (return on investment) from a brand-new client for an investment of £10, £20 or even £50 which you have spent on free copies of your book or newsletters is a pretty good return.

In my experience and the experience of my inner circle members, this certainly beats the return you will get from paying for Facebook likes or SEO work on your website.

That lifetime value described above doesn't include any additional products or services that you can sell that person over the time they remain a client. Which, if you keep delivering outstanding service to them, will hopefully be a very long time.

Technically, once you have a client and you keep delivering the goods, there is no reason they shouldn't remain a client for ever. The hard part is getting them to take that first step and commit to you in the first place.

That's why switching your marketing to a lead generation model like I described here is such a great idea. It's also where

I and most of the pet business owners I coach have their greatest successes too.

Lead generation is a much more measurable and targetable approach to building a client base (and a profitable business). Lead generation may not be as sexy as using Periscope or Twitter or whatever the latest new fad is on social media, but trust me, it works. I know because I use it to market all my dog businesses.

Lead generation is the road less travelled by most businesses, but as with anything in life, the majority are almost always wrong. Don't write lead generation marketing off as being too difficult to implement in your own dog walking business.

There's a lot to take in here.

I hope this book has intrigued you and inspired you to believe you can achieve much more with your business if you get your positioning right and have your marketing systems firing on all cylinders.

By launching your own business, you've stated that you want something different in your life than a job working for 'the man'. That is a big brave step, but it's just the first step. What comes after that is more important because not all businesses survive. In fact, 80% of all new businesses cease trading within five years, and you really don't want to be one of those statistics.

When you chose dog walking, you picked a profitable, popular and growing niche which shows no signs of slowing down. But sadly, you can't rely on just your dog walking and customer service skills to get your business to the top (and keep it there). Ultimately it will be the businesses who walk dogs brilliantly, treat their clients fabulously and market themselves effectively who are most likely to thrive and reach the heady heights of being the go-to dog walker in town.

Don't leave it to chance, though. Step up today, and as well as implementing the ideas I have shared with you in this book, you should commit to learning more about how to market your business effectively.

How far can you take your business?

In this book, I believe I have given you the key foundations that will help you better position your business so you can quickly be seen as the premier dog walker in your town (and if you agree, then please leave a review on Amazon for me).

In this secret sixth chapter, I also gave you an overview into lead generation marketing. You know how it works and why it's so effective, and you have lots of ideas you can swipe right now and implement in your own business.

What's next for you?

Marketing, much like dog training, is not a one-hit wonder, and you can't expect to learn everything you need to know in one book or course. I myself continue to invest in my marketing AND my dog training knowledge. Although it's the marketing training which makes me more money.

And there's a lot more for you to learn.

To have a true sales machine, you also need to know how to identify and attract your ideal client, how to build products and offers that your clients will buy, how to use referrals to grow your business, how to increase the range of products and services you have to offer so you can extract maximum value from every prospect who you turn into a client, how to build continuity into your business so you have more regular and predictable income, and how to automate your marketing and systemise your business so you can scale and grow beyond your current location – or even just how to take more time off to enjoy other aspects of your life, relaxed in the knowledge that your business is still ticking over and growing, even while you are not there to oversee everything.

So if you want it, then there's a lot more to learn, and to help you I have some more in-depth free training for you to enjoy.

Head to www.growyourpetbusinessfast.com and click on the free resources tab.

ABOUT THE AUTHOR

Dom Hodgson is an expert dog trainer, bestselling author and the most sought-after pet business coach in the UK.

With his eldest son, Alex, he runs the UK's number-one dog adventure company, Pack Leader Dog Adventures. Since 2011, PLDA has been helping dog owners in Sunderland have more fun and less stress with their dogs.

In 2016, Dom wrote the bestselling *How To Be Your Dog's Superhero*, which is available to buy from Amazon Kindle, as an audiobook on Audible or you can get a signed copy (and a special free gift) by going to
www.mydogssuperhero.com/getcopy

Walk Yourself Wealthy is just one of the business books in the 'Grow Your Pet Business FAST!' series. To find out more about Dom's other books, courses and pet business coaching you should go to www.growyourpetbusinessfast.com

Dom is an international speaker and teaches pet dog owners how to have more fun (and get more control) with their dogs and pet business owners how to have more fun (and make more money) in their business. To book Dom to come and speak at an event, you should email
dom@packleaderdogadventures.co.uk

Dom lives in Town Farm with his resident proofreader (and beautiful wife) Beth; youngest son, Toby; and their two dogs Sid the Cocker and Derek the Dogue de Bordeaux.

ACKNOWLEDGEMENTS

It took me the best part of a year to write my first book but a little over four months to write the next four. That's possibly due to the superb network of friends, mentors and loved ones who help me every step of the way.

First and always first comes my family.

Beth is by my side in everything I do, and I wouldn't get half (or even a quarter) of it done without her constant support. Toby and Alex are the best boys a dad could ask for and always make me proud (we have a great laugh too).

Alex also does an amazing job as the Adventure Operations Manager running Pack Leader Dog Adventures, which is the adventure and boarding side of our business. He is ably assisted by Dan Alberts, our Canine Fulfilment Officer, who also takes care of the training support within the Superhero Dog Owners Inner Circle.

My Mam and Dad are always there to help me and Beth with the kids, dogs and the business, so thanks again to you two. X

Huge thanks to my mentor Jon McCulloch and my fellow Elites for pushing me so hard this year. Without the Elite process I wouldn't be where I am now.

Thanks also to my good friend and resident expert for all things video, Alex 'the video guy' Wardle. Alex takes care of all my podcasts, events and online training videos, and I can't recommend him enough.

Thanks to my business buddies Ben Waters and Kathryn Reid and to the brilliant Vicky Fraser who I am cooking up another book with right now...

Thanks also to the wonderful Julia Brown who, I'm sure you agree, has designed another, rather splendid book cover. Thank you Julia!

And finally, thanks to you, of course, for buying and reading this book!

You are done. This is the end. Well not quite, because now you need to turn the page and claim your free gifts, which will help you plug all this positioning training into your own business.

Mentioned in this book and further reading:

How To Be Your Dog's Superhero – Dominic Hodgson

Business For Superheroes – Vicky Fraser

Grow Your Business FAST! – Jon McCulloch

101 Naked Confessions Of A Gay Hairdresser – Terry Wilson

No B.S. Marketing To The Affluent (or indeed any book written by) – Dan Kennedy

MY FREE GIFT TO YOU

Claim four powerful and profit-boosting free gifts now.

I want this book to represent a new start for your dog walking business.

Like you, I've read loads of books but most of them get shelved as soon as I've finished. In my life there have only been a dozen or so books that I've enjoyed enough for me to want to read them again. More importantly, I've only read a handful of books that have inspired me to take action on the content once I'd finished.

I want this to be one of those books for you, and my mission now is to get you to take action on what you have learned in *Walk Yourself Wealthy* .

Your business should be too important to you not to take action and start implementing the marketing secrets I have shared with you. I know for a fact (because I have done it myself) that you will be making more money a lot faster once you actually start.

So to help you get started, I have four special gifts for you.

1. Gift number 1 is an email marketing crash course. When I do my seminars and events, I always get questions about email marketing. In this seven-day email crash course, I will show you in more detail how you

68

can use email marketing as the perfect follow-up to turn your prospects into clients and grow your dog walking business, fast! To get this course, go to

www.growyourpetbusinessfast.com and click on the free resources tab.

2. Gift number 2 will help you kickstart your book-writing process. This is the book you will write that will catapult you above the competition and cement your expert status. 'Why your book is the best business card' is a one-hour audio training I did with top copy-writer and book coach, Vicky Fraser. Vicky and I talk about the what, and how you can write a book that will position yourself as the go-to dog walker in town. To get access to this audio, go to www.growyourpetbusinessfast.com and click on the free resources tab.

3. Gift number 3 is an hour-long Premium Pricing Masterclass that has only ever been seen by members of my 'Pet Business Inner Circle'. It will help you increase your prices without losing clients and help you better deal with objections from price buyers. To get exclusive access to this powerful training, go to www.growyourpetbusinessfast.com and click on the free resources tab.

4. And the fourth and final gift is a free subscription to my monthly paper-and-ink newsletter, 'The Pack Leader Business Gazette'. This profitable publication is essential reading for any ambitious pet professional. If you bought the book direct from me, then you will al-

ready be added to my mailing list, but if you are reading the Kindle version, listening to the audio book or got this book as a gift, then you can sign up today and I will mail this monthly business-building newsletter to you, for free. To activate your free subscription, go to www.growyourpetbusinessfast.com and click on the free resources tab.

You have in your hands a blueprint for success. There really is no excuse for you not to take one (or all) of these free resources to further build on what you have learned so far. The information in each one of these free gifts has the power to transform your business, but if you implement all of them, you have the potential to put your business growth on steroids.

How far you take your dog walking business is up to you. Is this going to be a hobby business that just pays the bills, or will it be the premium, profitable and fun dog walking empire you want it to be?

To get the answer to that question and more help from me, go to www.growyourpetbusinessfast.com and click on the free resources tab.

If you have trouble accessing any of these resources, then email me at dom@packleaderdogadventures.co.uk and I will be happy to sort it out.

Thanks for reading.

Keep it unreal.
Dom Hodgson

Made in United States
Orlando, FL
12 August 2023

36017684R00050